HOLIDAY FAVORITES

Solos and Band Arrangements
Correlated with Essential Elements® Band Method

Arranged by ROBERT LONGFIELD, JOHNNIE VINSON, MICHAEL SWEENEY and PAUL LAVENDER

Welcome to Essential Elements Holiday Favorites! There are two versions of each selection in this versatile book. The SOLO version appears in the beginning of each student book. The FULL BAND arrangement of each song follows. The ONLINE RECORDINGS or PIANO ACCOMPANIMENT BOOK may be used as an accompaniment for solo performance. Use these recordings when playing solos for friends and family.

To access audio visit:
www.halleonard.com/mylibrary
Enter Code
3706-0852-6636-8648

ISBN 978-1-5400-2803-7

HAL•LEONARD®

Visit Hal Leonard Online at
www.halleonard.com

00870021

Contact Us:
Hal Leonard
7777 West Bluemound Road
Milwaukee, WI 53213
Email: info@halleonard.com

In Europe contact:
Hal Leonard Europe Limited
42 Wigmore Street
Marylebone, London, W1U 2RN
Email: info@halleonardeurope.com

In Australia contact:
Hal Leonard Australia Pty. Ltd.
4 Lentara Court
Cheltenham, Victoria, 3192 Australia
Email: info@halleonard.com.au

AULD LANG SYNE

Words by ROBERT BURNS
Traditional Scottish Melody
Arranged by MICHAEL SWEENEY

3

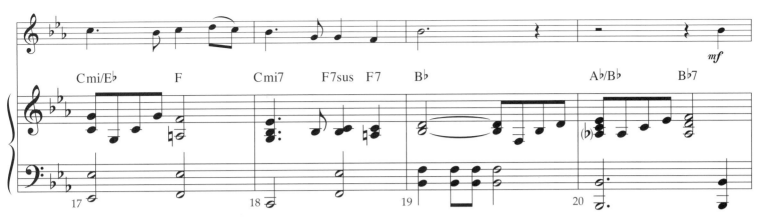

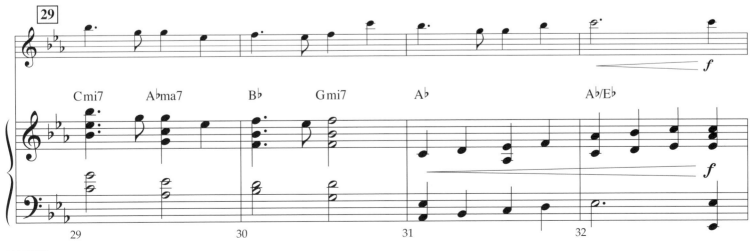

0087002100870021

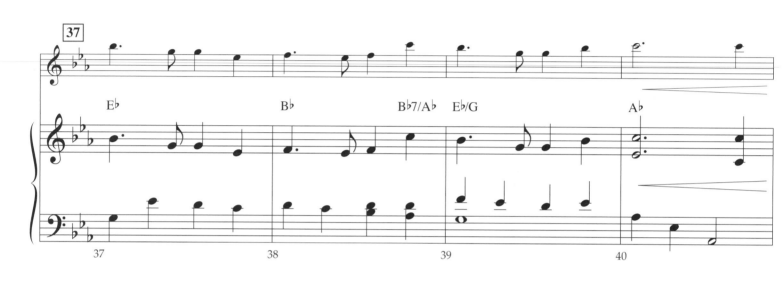

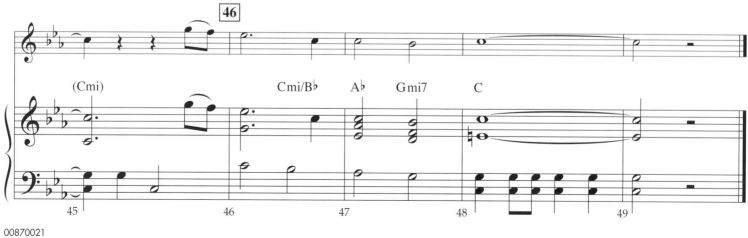

FELIZ NAVIDAD

Music and Lyrics by
JOSÉ FELICIANO
Arranged by PAUL LAVENDER

00870021

6

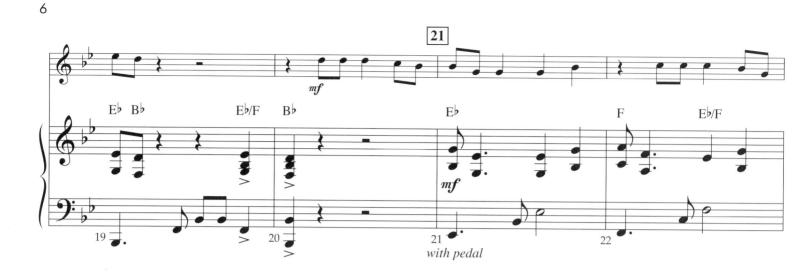

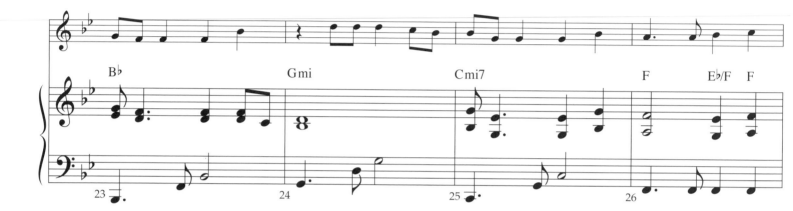

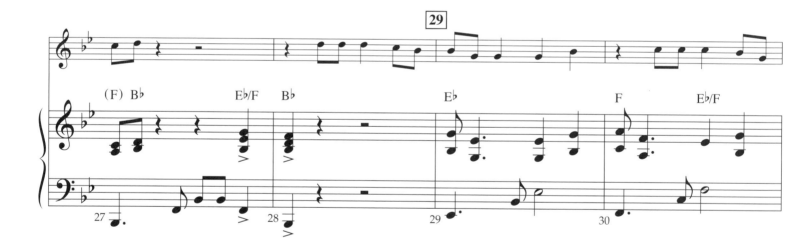

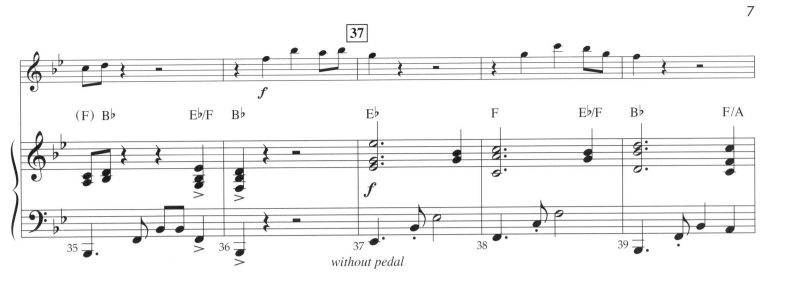

PARADE OF THE WOODEN SOLDIERS

English Lyrics by BALLARD MacDONALD
Music by LEON JESSEL
Arranged by PAUL LAVENDER

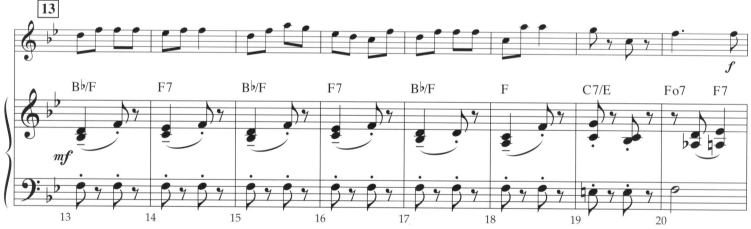

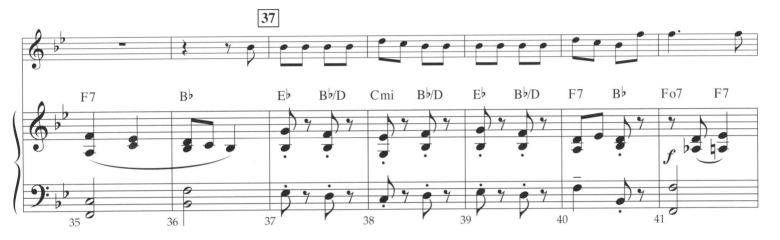

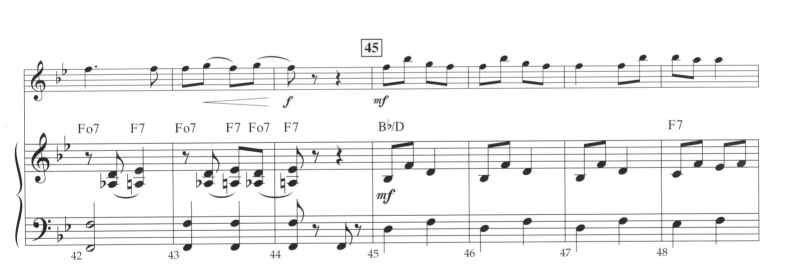

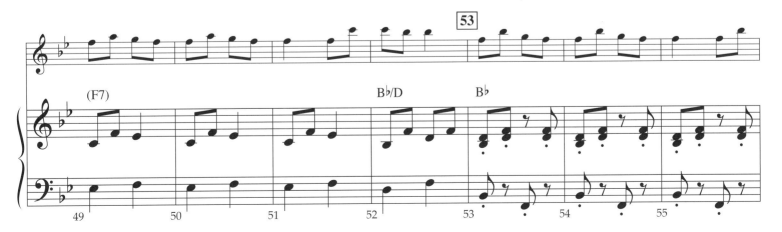

GOOD KING WENCESLAS

Words by JOHN M. NEALE
Music from PIAE CANTIONES
Arranged by ROBERT LONGFIELD

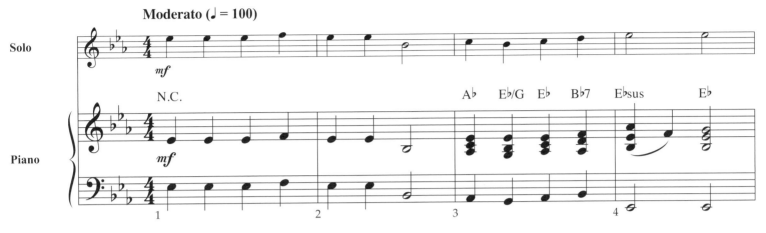

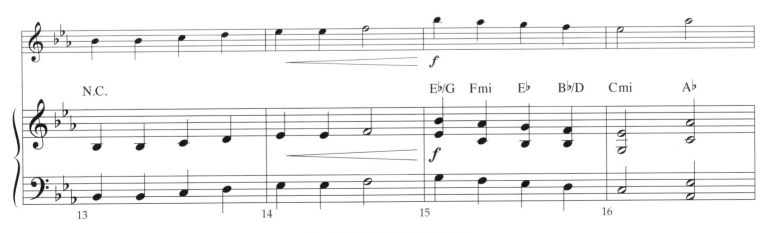

12

00870021

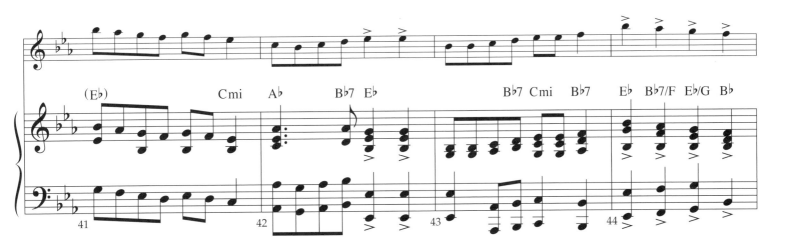

PAT-A-PAN
(Willie, Take Your Little Drum)

Words and Music by
BERNARD de la MONNOYE
Arranged by ROBERT LONGFIELD

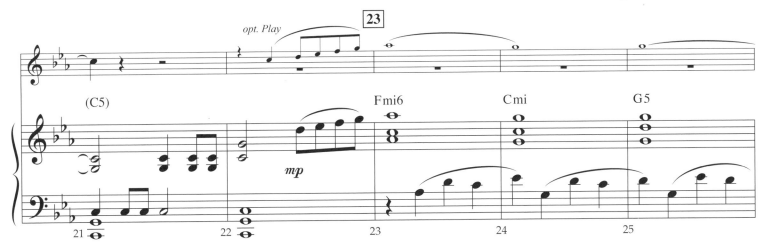

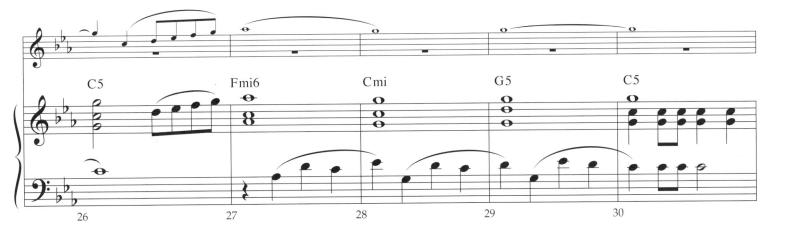

SILVER BELLS

**Words and Music by
JAY LIVINGSTON and RAY EVANS**
Arranged by PAUL LAVENDER

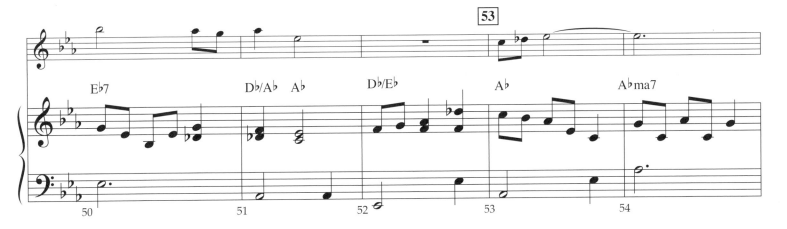

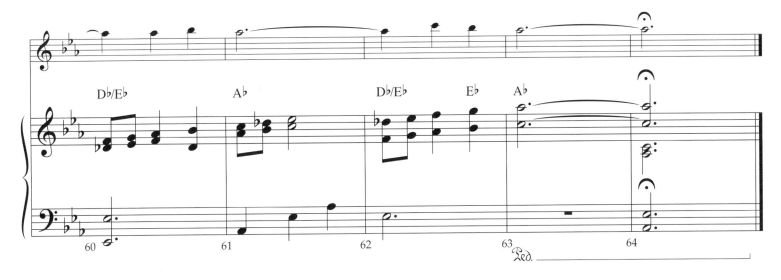

DO YOU HEAR WHAT I HEAR

**Words and Music by
NOEL REGNEY and GLORIA SHAYNE**
Arranged by MICHAEL SWEENEY

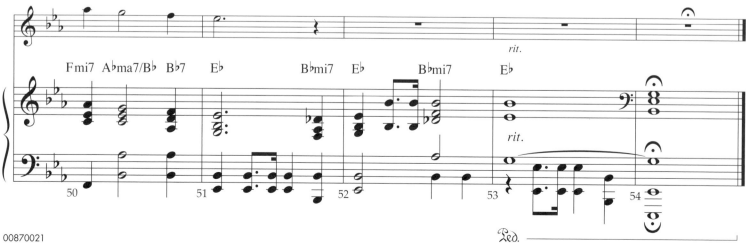

(This page left intentionally blank for a page turn.)

From THE SOUND OF MUSIC

MY FAVORITE THINGS

Lyrics by OSCAR HAMMERSTEIN II
Music by RICHARD RODGERS
Arranged by ROBERT LONGFIELD

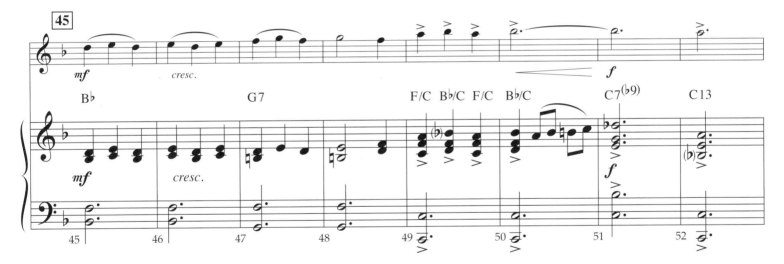

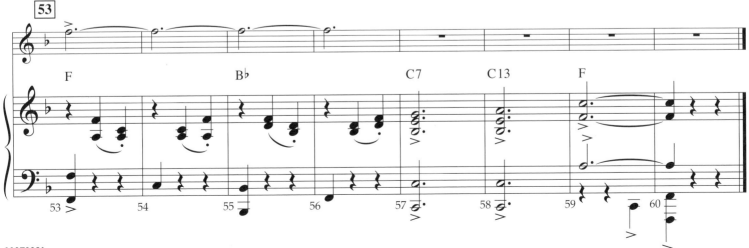

From the Motion Picture Irving Berlin's HOLIDAY INN

WHITE CHRISTMAS

Words and Music by
IRVING BERLIN
Arranged by JOHNNIE VINSON

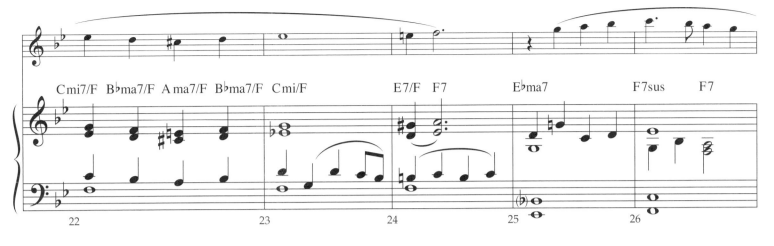

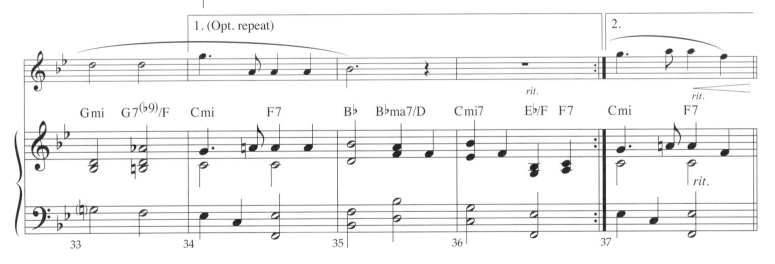

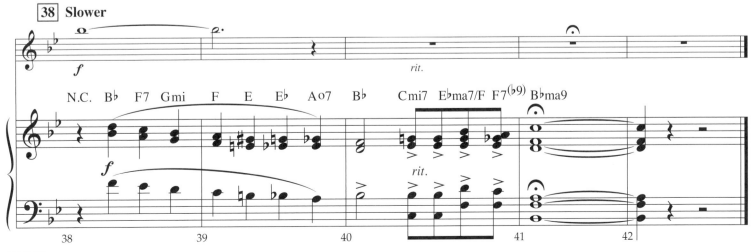

CHRISTMAS TIME IS HERE

Words by LEE MENDELSON
Music by VINCE GUARALDI
Arranged by JOHNNIE VINSON

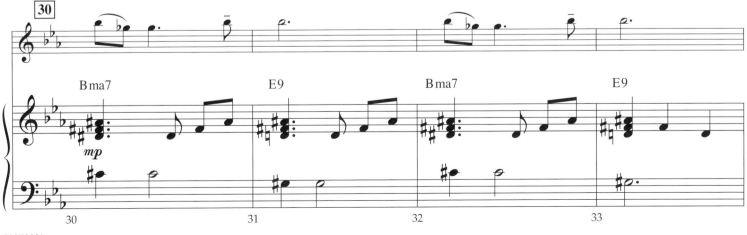

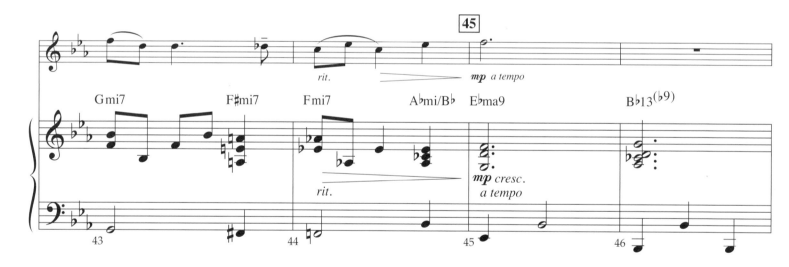

(This page left intentionally blank for a page turn.)

THE POLAR EXPRESS

Words and Music by
GLEN BALLARD and ALAN SILVESTRI
Arranged by JOHNNIE VINSON

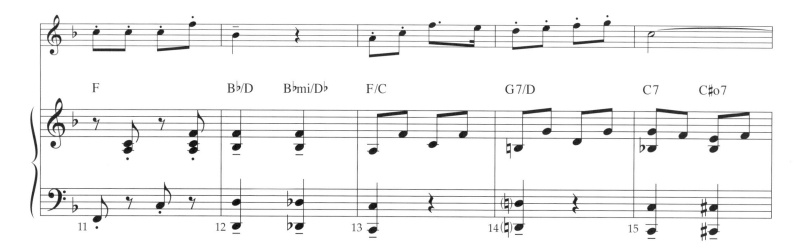

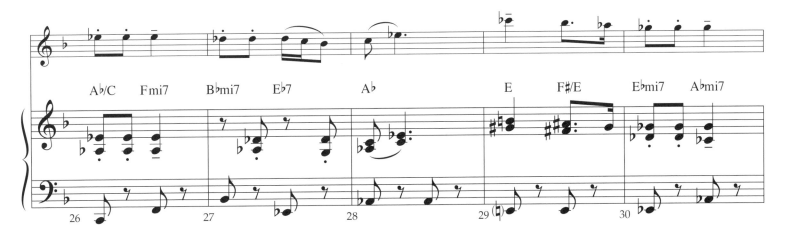

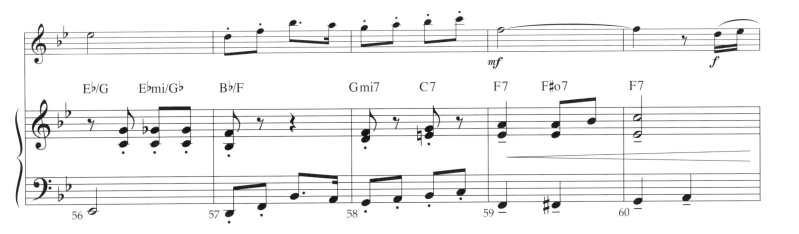

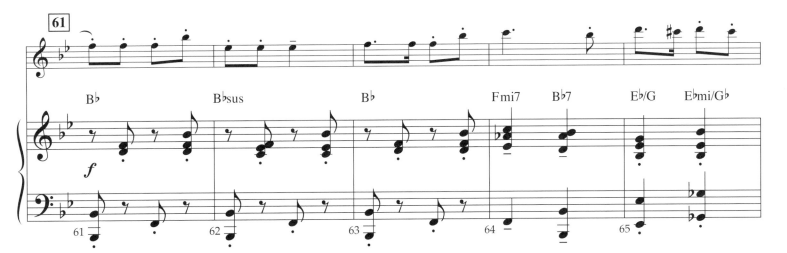

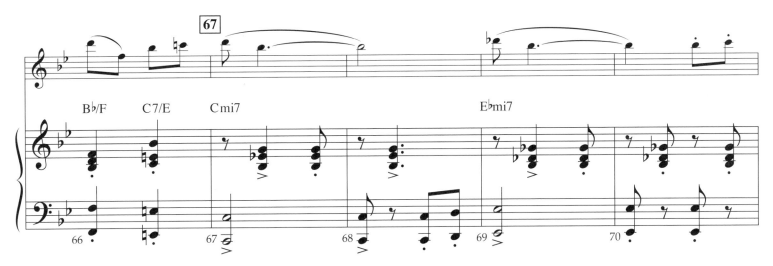

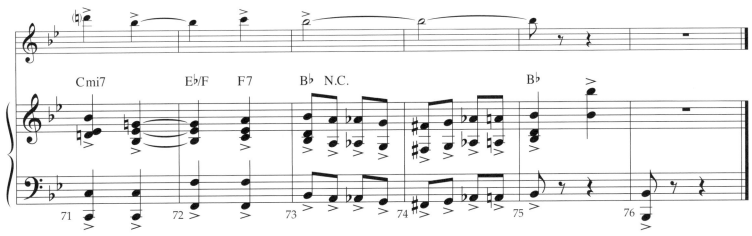